Find Your Passion

The Ultimate No-BS Workbook

186 Questions, Prompts, and Exercises to Find Your Passion, Work on

Purpose, and Leave a Lasting Legacy

GERALD CONFIENZA

A Gift for You

Most of the material I write about is centered on developing our inner selves. Thus, as you might've guessed, my readers are usually introverts. I can appreciate that because I'm an introvert myself. However, as an introvert, I'm also aware of our social shortcomings. This is why I have decided to gift you with some amazing material for your growth. By simply clicking the link below, you will have access to the *Introvert Survival Kit* and *Inward Thrive* Email Series for free.

Visit the following site or click here for full access: http://bit.ly/introvertsk

This powerful bundle will help you make massive improvements in your social life. It contains 3 Ebooks and 2 articles:

- EBook 1: Making and Keeping Friends: Developing Friendships that Last a Lifetime in this Fast Paced World!

- EBook 2: How to Stop Worrying and Start Living Effectively In the 21st Century: An Updated Guide to Living Free of Worry in the Knowledge Era

- EBook 3: High Impact Communication: Tips on Getting Your Strongest Message Across in 1 Minute

- Article 1: How to Break the Cycle of Anxiety and Enjoy Social Situations

- Article 2: Be an Introvert and Have an Active Social Life

Along with the material, you will also get a lot of bonus gifts in the days to come. I'd recommend not missing out! Just go to http://bit.ly/introvertsk

I also have a special invitation for those appreciate a good read. If you'd like to be part of the review process of many of our upcoming books (and receive free copies!) and click here: http://bit.ly/itadvancedreview I will send you details of what it entails through mail. Thanks!

Table of Contents

Introduction

Is it real? Is it even possible?

We've all seen the YouTube videos and occasional Facebook ads with extremely successful people encouraging you to find your passion, monetize it, and live the dream life- only to sell us something in the end. Deep inside we all want a life lived at its maximum expression and in constant expansion. The great problem is that we don't know where to start. There was never a *How to Find Your Passion 101* class in college! Lack of self-knowledge and lack of clarity of what we should be doing is the great problem of our generation. If you're feeling lost too, then let me tell you something:

I've been there too.

A few years ago, I was in college studying for a degree I knew I was never going to use. I knew that there had to be a way in which I could use my talents to bring value to the world and create economic and holistic abundance in my life. However, whenever I tried to start anything, my undertakings would be short-lived. I tried to push myself through willpower alone, but, in the end, I'd always end up leaving projects half-done. My self-esteem plummeted as I grew increasingly disappointed in myself. I couldn't find that calling for which I was made and the idea of living the dream life was slowly drifting from sight.

I was blessed that during this time I met a friend named Sebastian Harth. More than a friend, he became an early mentor in my life and introduced me to the world of personal development. One of the ideas he reiterates in his mentorships is the importance of finding your passion and purpose through self-discovery. I took heed to his words and, thus, began in me a process of self-discovery and self-actualization. It's only been 4 years since then, but my life has completely changed. When I met Sebastian, I had barely enough money to eat- extreme, I know. But it's the truth. I had begun a business that I was injecting all my money into. My diet consisted of fruits and bread; that's how financially broke I was. Today, I am proud to be indefinitely retired from the workforce. I live off passive income, do what I love, and have absolute control of where I take my life from here on out.

Advice is a very cheap commodity that you shouldn't receive from just anyone. To illustrate this, during my seminars I always give the example of the college MBA professor who advises his or her students on how to start a business, when they've never started one themselves. How sound can advise derived only from theory be? I, instead, am somebody who is reaping the benefits of having worked insatiably on their passion for the last 4 years. From a place of coherence, I will guide you through a process that I have applied on myself and hundreds of others that will help you find your passion and instruct you into massive action.

In the pages that follow, I have compiled a series of carefully designed questions, prompts, and exercises laid out in workbook format. Completing these will instigate self-knowledge at a visceral level, probably like you've experienced before. I ask that you keep an open mind. Skepticism is ignorance's best friend. Only when we come with an empty cup can we get our cup filled. Answer these questions thoroughly and with no filter, and the workbook will reveal things about you that you didn't know yourself. I guarantee that, at the very least, you will find your passion. I say very least because my hope is that you also find your personal mission and life purpose.

This Workbook Belongs to...

An Integrated System: Laying Foundations

Here's a secret of overachievers: they have an *integrated system*. What's this system about?

A few years ago, I found myself talking with the leading authority in Neuro-linguistic Programming in the Hispanic world, Edmundo Velasco. I had ended up in one of his seminars through the recommendation of a friend. It was 8 hours of intense sessions and I was gladly receiving way more than my money's worth in information. For those who don't know, Edmundo was a business partner of John Grinder, the co-founder of Neuro-linguistic Programming (a.k.a. NLP), a science predominantly used in success coaching that studies human behavior in relation to neural maps.

Immediately after the seminar, I approached Dr. Velasco for some quick Q&A. The conversation ended with a few answers and a promise I'd sign up for his NLP course the following week. A great journey into the workings of the human mind had begun.

I had always wanted to know what makes great people great. The answer soon came. Edmundo was starting an introduction of Robert Dilt's Neurological Levels of the mind when he commented, "success and human achievement is very predictable. You see, extremely successful people have one thing in common: they have a powerful and, more importantly, integrated mindset. They have a set of empowering beliefs and values that are in harmony with their life purpose. There's no room for self-sabotage".

A light bulb flicked inside my head. That's it! That's what I was looking for! I must've studied the material on developing an aligned, integrated mindset over a thousand times. I couldn't get enough.

As I continued my path in personal development and continued learning the workings of the human mind, I came across the same concept explained in diverse ways. Even World-class coach Tony Robbins teaches it in his seminars. I will explain it to you in the way that it was taught to me.

The Workings of the System

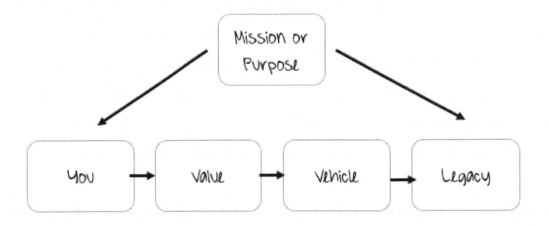

The system above is made up of 5 different parts:

1. Finding your passion first begins with finding a mission or purpose that you feel a need to accomplish. Everyone has one. Yes, you do too and if you haven't found it already, we will do so on the following pages.

   Everyone has something they can't die without having done or contributed towards. E.g. lift people up, especially those who have been emotionally scarred during childhood.

2. After finding a worthwhile mission or purpose for ourselves, we must identify who we are. What makes you *you*? As mentioned, we're made up of beliefs and conditioning. The way we define ourselves will play a huge role in the way we're going to take action towards our mission.

   E.g. If you're a die-hard introvert and your mission is to lift people up, then instead of going in front of crowds of tens of thousands to reach out to your audience, you may prefer to use your writing as a means of communication.

3. The next step that will help narrow down possibilities even further is taking values into consideration. In order to make sure our emotional and moral needs are met through our actions, values have to be identified. If not, we could be working towards our mission yet still be miserable doing it. What's important to you? What do you value?

   E.g. If one of your predominant values is leaving your comfort zone, then despite being an introvert, you may still want to practice becoming a better public speaker and developing your own personal speaking style to get your message across. If, on the other hand, you value recognition the least and value sending a powerful message above anything, you may prefer to continue writing but under a pen name. For some people, the use of a pen name is indispensable if they want to bare themselves and their ideas to the world without inhibition.

4. Finally, we get to the part you've been looking for- the vehicle. The vehicle is the specific action in which you will hone your skill and through which you will accomplish your mission or purpose. The vehicle could be a specific, job, career, business idea, hobby, cause, etc. The vehicle is the means by which you will transmute your desire, your values, your identity, your sense of mission into concrete action that will lead to concrete results.

    E.g. Perhaps it's time to hone your skills in writing. Perhaps it's time to get a job in a large corporation that sells coaching and treatment for those with severe depression. Perhaps you want to open an NGO and blog about your coaching endeavors. You must choose one among the many vehicles available.

5. There, you've found your passion! You've taken all the elements that make up *you* and transformed them into an action through which you can take your life to its maximum expression. Are we done? Not yet. There's one, tiny, final, yet very crucial step. Legacy. Legacy defines the life of a human being. This brings back memories of me watching the Disney Movie *Coco* with my girlfriend. In this movie, the dead live on in the afterlife as long as they're still remembered for the things they did in life. Once everyone has forgotten who they are, they pass on to the unknown. I thought it was a tremendous analogy- to measure the value of one's life by the legacy they've left behind. Excuse me for going off on a tangent. Anyways, legacy is where we can check if our course of action is really what we want. Ask yourself, "What do you want to be remembered for?"

    E.g. Perhaps for you it would be easier to find a job as a writer with work focused on helping others. However, you want to be remembered as someone more adventurous and entrepreneurial. Then, the logical choice would be to start your own business or NGO and focus on writing content that will add value to the life of thousands, if not millions.

Step 1: Finding Your Purpose

Easier said than done?

I think that's just an idea shared by people too lazy to look and search for information on their own. I don't think it's easy, but it's not hard either. Before we delve into finding your purpose, we'll clarify what purpose is not.

Your Purpose is Not...

Something you 'should' be doing. All our lives we've been told what to do and were forced into doing it whether we liked it or not. Remember that boring history class from 4th grade that had you grueling past the coursework the entire year? We've been conditioned to do things we don't want. We've also been conditioned to have decisions made for us. You know, the *go to school, get good grades, go to college, get a job, have kids, retire, and voila!* These are some of the key reasons as to why purpose is so elusive to many of us.

I'm not saying to *not* do any of the things mentioned above. I'm saying that you don't *have* to do them- it's not mandatory. Let me give you a hint: your purpose is never a *'should'* or a *'must'*. It's more of a *'want'*. This *'want'*, when fueled by decision and passion, eventually becomes a personal *'must'*. But, it always starts as a *'want'*. Martin Luther King Jr. was never obligated to fight for equal rights, he deeply wanted to. Actually, he was constantly told by his wife to stop, she knew what could happen if he continued. Despite his fear, Dr. King continued to live on purpose and eventually paid the ultimate price for the freedoms people of all races enjoy in the USA and around the world.

What Your Purpose Can Be

During a leadership summit, I heard the speaker say something that has stuck with me until today. "Life is God's gift to you. The way you live your life is your gift back to God". What a beautiful line. There's something I would add, though. It's not just the way you live your life, but the purpose you try to fulfill with it. *If you had to give up all your deeds in life as an offering to God (or to a force beyond yourself) and were evaluated by the positive change your deeds brought forth to creation (animals, people, planet, etc.), what would you want this change to be?*

What a Purpose-Filled Life Feels Like

Purpose is not a goal, it's the everyday living. Excuse the esoteric language, but I'm a firm believer that everything that happens to you in life happens for a reason. We've all heard this cliché, however, few of us actually question the events in our life (most just complain about them). *What am I supposed to learn from this? What is this event trying to show me about myself? How can I evolve from this event onwards?* These are the right questions to ask. Why? Because when you take into account your personal story, your childhood, your parents, your personal traumas, the traumas you've seen others overcome, your imperfection, your weaknesses, your strengths, your skills, your talents, your desires, your longings, your role models, etc., then you begin to see a pattern. You begin to see a mission or purpose only someone who has lived your life and experienced everything you've experienced could do.

So, what does purpose feel like? It feels like *alignment*. It feels like congruence. It feels like wholeness. Above all there is certainty- that there's nothing else in the world you could be or should be doing other than *this*.

In the End, We Make Up Our Own Legend

Human beings are makers of history because we are makers of stories. Make up a story about yourself until it's one you feel congruent with. Until it's one that sums up everything that is *you*. That is what we will do with the following questions (and throughout the rest of the book). Enjoy the process!

Questions for Finding Your Purpose

In the following pages, you will encounter dozens of questions that will help you find your *purpose*. Answer them in detail and write as much as you can. Let your hand move on its own for once.

Finding Your Purpose: 57 Questions, Prompts, and Exercises

1. What would I change about the world, if I knew I could not fail?

2. At the end of my life, what would I most regret not having done?

3. If you knew that you will die 5 years from now, what would you spend your remaining life doing?

4. Describe a life that you would only have in nightmares. Sometimes knowing what we don't want helps us find what we want.

5. Why do I admire my role models?

6. Over the last month, when have you felt most motivated, inspired, and in a state of absolute focus? What were you doing? Who were you being?

7. What makes you happy? Yup, list everything.

8. If I could be granted the power to change the world, what would I do?

9. If my heart could talk, what would it say my purpose in life was?

10. What change brought forth to the lives of others by me would make me cry with joy, or brings tears to my eyes?

11. What is a horrible experience you would like to protect others from at all costs?

12. If my heart could talk, it would tell me to... (Hint: Describe actions you could take now)

13. What causes do you strongly believe in or connect with?

14. What perks up my curiosity?

15. What is something you've gone through and wish no one else ever had to? What is one thing someone should never have to experience?

16. What is the greatest and most memorable act of kindness a stranger has ever done for you? What would you say to that stranger?

17. Who in history would I most love to be, and why?

18. The world could change completely if people were to...

19. The greatest ideal people can dedicate their lives to is...

20. What would you tell your grandkids 50 years from now that you were the proudest of in your life?

21. As a kid, what are you about? Before any seriousness or ambition snuck in? Which memories most electrify your body/mind when you think of them?

22. What are the greatest problems you have encountered in your life? In overcoming them, what talents, gifts, and ideas have you developed?

23. How does you having lived on Earth and existed make humanity better?

24. What is the most important thing in my life?

25. If I had to make my best guess of my life's purpose, what would it be?

26. What would you like to have received help or mentorship with growing up? What was a hardship you wish someone would've helped you overcome?

27. What have I always been insecure about? What is one thing I could never overcome about myself?

28. What would you regret dying without having contributed towards?

29. What would I like to leave the world, as my legacy?

30. Over the last seven days, what moments have given you feelings of great love, deep satisfaction, or purpose?

31. What does triumph mean to you?

32. It's been over 100 years after your death. What impact your life has had on society is still felt today?

33. If I had to get started with something that would push me towards my life's purpose, what would it be?

34. What is one thing no one should die without having had experienced?

35. What do you want your epitaph to be?

36. Who are you most grateful for in your life? Make a list of those people and describe why.

37. What are you willing to pay the ultimate price for? What change would you like to see around you that you'd be willing to work day and night for?

38. What does legacy mean to you?

39. What qualities do my role models possess that I'd also like to be known for?

40. How would I define the life purpose of my role models?

41. You, your family, and your loved ones have all the time and money in the world. What would you dedicate your life to?

42. What challenge would I love to overcome, and then help others achieve the same?

43. Would 8-year-old you be proud of who you are today? What would he recommend that you do?

44. What do I most regret not doing, so far in my life?

45. What is the best way to help somebody else? Financially? Emotionally? Physically? Spiritually? Why?

46. What has been the greatest challenge that I have overcome so far in my life? Could I help other people to overcome that same challenge?

47. What special gift do I have that I could give to the world?

48. What do I want to insatiably learn about?

49. Who are the people I most admire for the legacy they've left behind?

50. What does *love* mean to you?

51. Perform a word-association exercise with the word purpose. When you're done, look over the list of words you've created. Is there a common theme? Or perhaps a mood? Freewrite for ten minutes regarding what you notice about your list.

52. Design a purpose-based vision board. In a wall or cardboard, pin down images and photos of what you want to see in your life. Make sure that what you're putting down is something that motivates you into action.

53. If you had to find images and photos that describe the contributions you would make to the world, what images would you collect? What images do you hold in your head and in your heart that sum up the life you want to live? How can you project the legacy you want to leave behind through these images? Make sure to add these images to the vision board assignment described above.

54. Ask your parents or a guardian who took care of you as a child. Ask them what cause 6-8yr old you would've loved to lead.

55. Find someone who you admire for the change he or she is making to his community, city, state, or country. Reach this person through phone or mail and ask him or her how they found their life purpose. Ask them to help you find yours.

56. Attend a leadership and legacy seminar or certification. This may imply a heavy cost but it's small compared to the value you'll get from it. Knowing your purpose in life has no value. The John Maxwell Team or any Anthony Robbins seminar are both great starting points.

57. Having completed all the previous questions, prompts, and exercises please narrow down your purpose to 5 purpose statements, by completing the affirmation: *My purpose in life is…* Having completed this, narrow your purpose further down to only one statement. It doesn't have to be perfect, it only has to feel right.

Step 2: Finding Yourself

Here's some short piece of wisdom everyone should incorporate into their lives by Socrates himself: *"Know thyself"*. I think we can all agree that all of wisdom and achievement begins first from knowing who you are at a visceral level.

Why?

Knowing who you are allows you to truly develop self-love and acceptance of who you are. Being able to see past your imperfections and embrace your strengths marks the beginning of self-esteem, and self-esteem is necessary for any great achievement. Look at a list of all of humanity's greatest achievers and you will find men and women with incredible self-esteem.

Salvador Dalí, easily the most prominent painter of the 20th century, was a Spanish surrealist with an uncanny sense of self-esteem. He was found routinely talking to himself in third person, addressing himself as you would address royalty. *"Does Master Dalí fancy some tea?"* He'd ask himself out loud when offered tea by hosts of parties and events. *"No, Master Dalí does not wish for tea"*, he'd reply. Yeah, pretty bizarre. He truly believed he was royalty, and that's probably why he painted like one.

If you know yourself, everything that makes you *you*, then decisions will come easily for you. Decisions are the shapers of your destiny. Recall a decision you made long ago that changed your entire life. Imagine what you'd be doing right now had you taken a different path. Actually, you need not go that far back. The decision to have purchased this workbook and the decision to complete it will set you off on a completely different path than if you had chosen to watch TV instead. See what I mean?

Who Am I?

Finding who you are, however, seems like no easy task. *Who am I?* is a question that has boggled the minds of the wisest men in history. As I'm clearly out of my league in making any contributions to this matter, I propose that we approach this topic from a psychological perspective and with a model that has shown results in the past. I'm referring to Robert Dilt's Logical Levels Model. Let me explain.

According to Robert Dilts, people's actions and results are made up of a logical mental model (or system) that's structured hierarchy. The more conscious, or aware, of we are of our psyche, the more superior logical levels we identify with. In short, when people are faced with the question, *who am I?* they will respond using any of the 7 subsets of logical levels you see in the image below.

Taken from http://www.management-learning.co.uk/single-post/2016/10/25/The-two-most-dangerous-words-for-managing-change

It's important to note from the image that a sense of purpose or mission that goes beyond ourselves (the one at the top) eventually defines the rest of what makes us who we are. This is why extremely successful people are more likely to define themselves by their mission rather than by their job position or their talents (and it's the first thing we did at the start of this workbook).

Why is This Important?

Knowing where we fit in the lower levels can allow us to use our strengths to our advantage when working towards our purpose, and/or help us change and adapt to varying beliefs, values or behaviors, if necessary. This is of crucial importance because many times we narrow down *'our passion'* to a simple skill or capability. This is a terrible mistake. The truth is that it's a bit more complicated.

We may be skilled at playing, *e.g.*, tennis, and may find success in this sport, however, if our values, sense of identity, and purpose are not aligned with this activity, then we'll never find any lasting fulfillment in its practice. The opposite is true as well. We may have no particular talent for the sport, but if we have a *burning desire* (purpose) to, *e.g.*, help people develop confidence in themselves, *identify* ourselves as givers of empowerment, and *believe* we can achieve anything we put our mind to, then, even if we lack the talent, we can *learn* professional tennis and use our success as a means of inspiration for the masses. In the latter case, we have identified where we fit in highest logical levels and this knowledge has pushed us into developing a skill to a professional level.

Stop Defining Your Passion Solely as An Activity, It's Much More Than That

Let me elaborate. Many people believe they have no talents at all and therefore stop their search for their passion. If you're one of those, then let me tell you something: it doesn't matter at all you have tons of talents or have none. Yup, you read me right. What matters is *why* and *for what purpose* you'd be willing to learn new skills or talents. *Purpose is the catalyst of all great achievements.*

Questions to Find Yourself

Well, it's time for you to find *you!* Join me for the following questions, prompts and exercises to identify *who you are* at each of the logical levels. As in the first section of the book we already covered purpose-based questions, questions here will focus on the lower levels: identity, beliefs/values, capabilities, behaviors and environmental.

Finding Who You are: 100 Questions, Prompts, and Exercises

Environment Level

Humans are creatures made to adapt to their environment. Our environment, whether we like it or not, shapes us in certain ways. Therefore, our first step in getting to know ourselves is identifying *how* our environment is dictating the way we behave and think. In this section, we will focus mostly on evaluating our inner circle of influence, perhaps one of the most important external factors that can make or break us.

1. Where do you spend the most time\Where do you like to spend the most time? Why?

2. Where would you like to spend the most time? Why?

3. Where wouldn't you like to spend any time at all? Why not?

4. Where do you your friends and family fit in your life? Do you prefer spending time with either group over the other? Why?

5. I love to spend time with people who…

6. What kind of people do you surround yourself with?

7. Why do you spend time with them?

8. Do you think that the people you spend the most time with at the moment add value to your life? Or do they take away from you?

9. Late success psychology expert Jim Rhon once said, *"you are the average of the 5 people you spend the most time with"*. Make a list of the 5 people you spend the most time with. Next to their names, add in adjectives and values that they hold and embody. Do these describe you as well? Next, pick out these adjectives and values and hand them to somebody you know. Ask them if these values and adjectives describe *you*. What's their opinion?

10. Having completed the exercise above, do you agree or disagree with Jim Rhon?

11. Having concluded the exercise above, we will proceed to do the same but under different criteria. Evaluate each one of the five people you spend the most time in a scale from 1-10 in the area of relationships, personal finances, spirituality, health, and results in life (results related to their own purpose). Next, do the same with you. Do you see any similarities?

12. Would you change the people that you spend the most time with? Or are you happy with the results? This question is necessary as the most common problem people face when starting anything new is resistance from their inner circle. Most people have never evaluated their inner circle before and have inadvertently let in toxic individuals into their life. Thus, it's quite common to find individuals with dreams and ambitions who are left paralyzed by the discouragement of those closest to them.

13. If it's necessary to change your inner circle, please list the predominant qualities you'd love for your inner circle to have.

Behavioural Level

Now it's time to look at the way we behave and our reactions to external stimuli. By understanding our behaviour, we can begin to analyse areas of strength and areas in need of improvement. Remember that anything at this level in the logical level pyramid can be easily changed. Don't be afraid to be honest with your answers to the following questions.

14. How do you handle difficult situations?

15. What do you do when your priorities change quickly? Describe a situation when this occurred and detail your reaction?

16. What your first reaction when you lose control of something that matters to you?

Ambition

17. How have you demonstrated your willingness to work hard in your previous endeavors? If not, what would you say the reason was?

18. What were (are) your study patterns in school? Describe a time when you work relentlessly to achieve an objective.

19. What project, job, or undertaking are you proud of having completed? What did it consist of? How hard did you work to achieve it?

20. Do you prefer getting things done without supervision? Why or why not?

21. Do you work harder with or without supervision? Why or why not?

22. What is the biggest risk you've taken in the past when following your gut? Detail your undertaking.

23. Describe an ideal challenge you'd like to take on?

24. Are details more your thing? Or do you prefer focusing on broad, big-picture objectives?

25. Recall a time where you had to work on details to get the job done. How did you feel about working on details? Is it something you'd like to de again?

26. Imagine you're the CEO of a large corporation. Would you be strict on following procedure? Or would you prefer to give employees more freedom in decision-making according to personal discretion? What does this say about your behavior in social groups?

27. Do you prefer to act leveraging powerful emotions in your favor? Or do you prefer to act after analyzing all possible solutions? What does this tell you about your decision-making process?

28. Recall a time you had to deal with someone who was extremely angry at you. How were you able to communicate with them? Were you able to get your message across?

29. Are you likely to make more friends out of people you approached or are all friends of yours part of your extended inner circle?

30. What do you do when you want to genuinely connect with others?

31. What about when you want to connect them to your cause? Is there any way this could be improved?

32. Teamwork, in my opinion, is…

33. Leadership, in my opinion, is…

34. How do you act when your part of a group as opposed to when you're on your own?

Which do you prefer?

Getting Results

35. Do you engage in goal-setting? Why or why not?

36. What would your choice of motivation be, if you had to create an incentive for your team to perform?

37. Describe the steps someone has to take to overcome challenges in their life.

38. Do you prefer to work to please those around you or would you rather do something for the good of everyone around you even if it gets you on their bad side?

39. What are you more likely to do, plan every detail of a project before taking action, or take action even if you only have a minimum amount of information? How is this pattern of behavior dictating the results you currently have? Is there any correlation? Why or why not?

40. How do you get around doing things that are not mandatory?

41. Do you prefer working harder or working smarter? How could you combine both to achieve bigger results?

42. When you say you're busy, is it because you're focusing on things that are important or urgent? Note that, *e.g.*, going to a routine medical checkup could be *urgent* (if it's already on your agenda for the day), but reading a book or meeting up with mentors that could help you get started on your purpose could be far more *important* for your life.

43. Are the things that you're doing on a daily basis getting you closer to your end goal? If not, how can you fix it?

44. In a scale from 1-10, how much do your emotions get in the way of you getting things done? How can we begin to use our emotions as leverage to get more done instead?

Communication

45. Are you more likely to listen or talk during one on one conversations?

46. How comfortable do you feel communicating unpleasant things to others or superiors?

47. Describe how you would get a group of people to join your cause.

48. In an argument, are you more willing to compromise or do you choose to impose your point of view to the very end?

49. Ever had difficulty speaking up? Describe a situation that left you nervous to speak up. Why did you feel this way?

50. How willing are you to take accountability and say *'I'm sorry'*?

51. How good do you consider yourself building rapport with others?

Skills and Capabilities Level

In finding your purpose in life, knowing what skills and capabilities you're already equipped with is of tremendous importance. In the following questions, we will narrow down your talents and skills and identify areas of expertise you may want to develop.

What have you always wanted to get good at? Great talent is not always something you're born with, most times it's something you develop.

52. Make a list of 25 things you think you're good at.

53. Make a list of 25 things that you like doing the most (except things like *eating* or *sleeping*).

54. What's a common denominator in the jobs, classes or assignments you've had in the past that you love?

55. What activities make you lose track of time (again, no sleeping, no scrolling past newsfeeds, etc)?

56. What activities did you indulge in as a kid? What kept you so engaged in them?

57. Grab your mom or guardian who raised you as a child. What did they think you'd end up growing up to be? What talents did they identify in you from a young age?

58. What did you love to do as a teen?

59. According to you, what are your greatest strengths?

60. According to a close family member, what are your greatest strengths?

61. According to a colleague or professor, what are your greatest strengths?

62. What topic or skill do others ask for your help in?

63. Make a list of activities that make you feel energized.

64. What topic sparks up your curiosity and makes you want to learn more about it?

65. What would you learn insatiably about?

66. What activities get you in a state of *flow*?

67. If you were to wake up tomorrow feeling free and excited about the upcoming day, what activities would this day be full of?

68. Intrinsically, do you feel that you were born to do any one thing?

69. What would you even if you weren't paid to do it?

Values and Beliefs Level

In this section, we will identify values and beliefs that have shaped the way you have lived life until now. In the questions that follow, we will also adjust the beliefs and values we have so that we may achieve more. We will start with values and continue with beliefs.

Values: The following exercise is taken directly from *Mindtools.com*. Please visit the following link on their site for the full article: http://bit.ly/FindingValues. Gauging what's important to you is of utmost importance for finding the way you'll choose to express your purpose. Values define you and are the base for the decisions you will make in your life. The way you will find expression of your identity and fulfill your purpose is extremely dependent on your core values. Take your time answering the following questions.

Part 1- Identifying Times When You Were Happy: Try to base your answers both on your personal and professional life.

70. What were you doing?

71. Were you with other people? Who?

72. What other factors contributed to your happiness?

Step 2: Identify the times when you the proudest: Base your answers both on your personal and professional life.

73. What other factors contributed to your happiness?

74. Why were you proud?

75. Did other people share your pride? Who?

76. What other factors contributed to your feelings of pride?

Step 3: Identify the times when you were most fulfilled and satisfied: Base your answers on your personal and professional life.

77. What need or desire was fulfilled?

78. How and why did the experience give your life meaning?

79. What other factors contributed to your feelings of fulfillment?

Step 4: Determine your top values: Base this on your experiences of happiness, pride, and fulfillment. This is easily one of the most important exercises for self-discovery you'll probably ever do. From the following list of values, pick only ten.

Acceptance	Contribution	Expressive
Achievement	Control	Fairness
Accountability	Conviction	Family
Adaptability	Cooperation	Famous
Alertness	Courage	Fearless
Altruism	Courtesy	Feelings
Ambition	Creation	Focus
Amusement	Creativity	Freedom
Assertiveness	Credibility	Friendship
Attentive	Curiosity	Fun
Awareness	Decisiveness	Generosity
Balance	Dedication	Genius
Beauty	Dependability	Giving
Boldness	Determination	Goodness
Bravery	Devotion	Grace
Brilliance	Dignity	Gratitude
Calm	Discipline	Greatness
Certainty	Discovery	Growth
Challenge	Drive	Happiness
Charity	Effectiveness	Hard work
Cleanliness	Efficiency	Harmony
Clever	Empathy	Health
Commitment	Empower	Honesty
Communication	Endurance	Honor
Community	Energy	Hope
Compassion	Enjoyment	Humility
Competence	Enthusiasm	Imagination
Concentration	Equality	Improvement
Confidence	Ethical	Independence
Connection	Excellence	Individuality
Consciousness	Experience	Innovation
Contentment	Exploration	Inspiring

	Potential	Spontaneous
Integrity	Power	Stability
Intelligence	Productivity	Status
Intensity	Professionalism	Stewardship
Intuitive	Prosperity	Strength
Irreverent	Purpose	Structure
Joy	Quality	Success
Justice	Realistic	Support
Kindness	Recognition	Surprise
Knowledge	Recreation	Sustainability
Lawful	Reflective	Talent
Leadership	Respect	Teamwork
Learning	Responsibility	Thoughtful
Liberty	Restraint	Timeliness
Logic	Results-oriented	Tolerance
Love	Reverence	Toughness
Loyalty	Rigor	Traditional
Mastery	Risk	Tranquility
Maturity	Satisfaction	Trust
Meaning	Security	Truth
Moderation	Self-reliance	Understanding
Motivation	Selfless	Unity
Openness	Service	Valor
Optimism	Sharing	Victory
Order	Significance	Vigor
Organization	Silence	Vision
Originality	Simplicity	Vitality
Passion	Sincerity	Wealth
Patience	Skill	Winning
Peace	Smart	Wisdom
Persistence	Solitude	Wonder
Playfulness	Spirituality	

80. Make a list of the 10 values that most resonate with you in this list.

81. Rank the 10 values in order from least important to you, to most important. The value ranked at the top is your essence.

Step 6: Reaffirm your values. Check your top-priority values, and make sure that they fit with your life and your vision for yourself.

82. Do these values make you feel good about yourself?

83. Are you proud of your top three values?

84. Would you be comfortable and proud to tell your values to people you respect and admire?

85. Do these values represent things you would support, even if your choice isn't popular, and it puts you in the minority?

Beliefs: Beliefs dictate a lot about our lives. Ever had the problem of not being able to get yourself to do something? Or finally doing it and end up sabotaging yourself? The greatest asset in our power as humans is our belief system. However, they can also be our greatest liability if left unattended. In this section, we will identify our empowering beliefs and limiting beliefs and begin a process of change.

86. What 3 negative thoughts/beliefs do you have that set you back the most?

87. Why do you have those beliefs? Make your answer as long as it needs to be. Take your time as you probe around for answers.

88. Rate each limiting belief from 1 to 10, with one being the least limiting and 10 being the most limiting. Which of your beliefs is the one that limits you the most? Why?

89. How have these limiting belief drained you in life? How have they held you back? Describe the pain having these beliefs has caused you.

90. If you let go of these limiting belief, what would happen? How would it transform your life? Please detail changes in your life that would happen individually for each of the 3 beliefs.

91. What's the worst that can happen if you were to act despite your limiting beliefs? Is it as bad as you've made seen in your brain? Do this exercise for all three limiting beliefs.

92. Each of the three limiting beliefs is stopping you from high achievement in their respective areas of your life. If you didn't have these limiting beliefs, what goals would you set for yourself in these areas of your life? How high would you aim?

93. Detail circumstances in which each of the limiting beliefs you've mentioned have been proved wrong. *E.g.*, if your limiting belief is that it takes money to make money, then can you come up with an example of a millionaire who started out in absolute poverty?

94. If you were to put your limiting belief on *hold* for a week (imagine it didn't exist) and chose to act is if you didn't have it, what would you do? Do this exercise for all three limiting beliefs?

95. Assign an area of your life to where each of these limiting beliefs reside (e.g. '*I am not good looking*' could be assigned under *Love $ Relationships*). Now, set for yourself a challenging goal in this area of your life. Remember that we're putting our limiting beliefs *on hold*, so it's okay to act as if you didn't have them. What 3 baby steps can you start taking right now to make that goal a reality?

96. This one may take a while, but I promise you that your life will be thoroughly enriched from completing the following exercise. I want you to take the remaining space on the page and divide it into 5 parts (like a pie chart). Each slice of the pie will represent one area of your life: Love (relationships, including family and friends), Wealth, Health, Results (Personal Achievement), Spirituality. In each one of these areas, write down 3 limiting beliefs that have held you back.

97. As a follow up to the previous exercise, please design a similar pie chart with the five areas of your life. Now, instead of writing down 3 limiting beliefs, write down 3 empowering beliefs you'd like to adopt in each of these areas.

Identity Level

Identity: This one's a tough one. At an identity level, we are the sum of the answers you've written thus far and much, much, more. Though few people hardly change at this level throughout their lives, it's quite possible to do it. I've encountered many people that, though they grew up in a horrible environment and adopted numerous limiting beliefs growing up (such as *'I'm worthless'*), desperately saw to change that and began working on their mind. If you asked them who they are today, they'd say something along the lines of *'I'm an ordinary human being with an extraordinary sense of purpose'*. My friend Henry is such case. He grew up in very poor living conditions and with little self-esteem. One day his life changed when he met a successful individual who lent him a hand, gifted him a book, and encouraged him to believe in himself. Henry developed the insatiable desire to become like this man. Today, Henry travels the world, is financially free, has more friends than he could count, and has become his family's pride and joy.

Henry's example has taught me that you should not define yourself only by who you are at this moment, but also by what you want to become. In the end, humans are the architects of their destiny. Therefore, I have only two prompts in this section: the former will get you writing about who you are right now, and the latter will get you writing about who you desperately want to become.

98. Who is (insert your name here)? In third person (using he/she, not me/I), write who (insert your name here) is. What is he or she about? What's their essence like? Spend the rest of the page writing about this very important person.

99. Now, final question. Who or what does (insert your name here) want to become? What's his or her ideal self? Spend the rest of the page detailing the future (insert your name here).

Purpose Level

Purpose: It all goes back to this: the purpose to which we'll dedicate our lives to fulfill. Luckily for us, we've already completed this part at the beginning of the workbook. If for some reason you haven't already, smack yourself in the head and go back to square one.

Step 3: What Do You Value?

We've identified our purpose, we know who we are, now it's just time to find our values. For this, please refer back to questions 71 through 86 *Self Discovery @ the Values and Beliefs Level*. By questions 86, you should've already found the values that most resonate with you, ranked the top 10 from least important to most important, and have identified your #1 value. Are you in agreement with what you found? What could be modified?

Make sure to have these fresh in your mind as they will be crucially important for the next step in this process of finding your passion- *choosing the right vehicle.*

Step 4: Choosing Your Vehicle

When people start their search for their passion, this is the level at which most stay. This is why people have such a tough problem deciding what to do in life. They're trying to choose a job, career, or business that is right for them, without having first considered what *'right'* is and who *they* really are.

Well, first things first. What's a vehicle? *A vehicle is a means by which you can reach your purpose, through the expression your identity, staying within the boundaries of your values, and making full use of your skills and capabilities.* It's what people will actually see you doing.

Finding Your Vehicle: 26 Questions, Prompts, and Exercises

Climbing the Career Ladder vs Diving into Entrepreneurship

The first thing we must do is find if you have entrepreneurial qualities in you. Being your own boss is becoming more and more accessible due to opportunities found on the internet, MLM companies, and even in the traditional business world. Your true calling may be found here. If it's not, however, rest at ease. Many people would rather avoid the unnecessary risk and grind of the entrepreneurial world and, instead, focus on perfecting their craft. That's valid as well.

In this section, we will identify the vehicle you will use to fulfill your purpose. First, we will evaluate if you have entrepreneurial tendencies through the *Entrepreneur Test*. Afterward, we will guide you through a list of questions to determine the vehicle (in the entrepreneur world or the career world) that will be most suitable for you.

Entrepreneur Test

1. Are you willing to pay the price? Entrepreneurship comes at a huge cost (not just monetary!), that you must pay out before seeing any results. This includes hardly getting in any sleep for a while, having people not believe in you, having others saying you're crazy and having you doubt yourself constantly.

2. Are you willing to start a process of never-ending learning and growth? Though this is true for any person living out their purpose, it's especially true for entrepreneurs because they will have to find mentors and adopt new habits early on if they want to see any progress.

3. Do you prefer to be a loner, or do you prefer working in groups? John C. Maxwell says that *"One is too small a number to achieve greatness"*. Entrepreneurs must be willing to recruit others into their business and be able to delegate work to leverage their actions. If you prefer working on your own, entrepreneurship may not be for you.

4. Do you like to sell? Or does the mere thought of it make you cringe? Every business must sell to survive. If leadership is the top quality that makes or breaks entrepreneurs, then selling is a close second. That brings me to the next question…

5. Are you a leader? Or are you willing to develop leadership qualities? Great businessmen are great leaders. Leadership is influence, nothing more and nothing less. The ability to influence your partners, your stakeholders, your workers, your clients, etc., is indispensable if you want to achieve great things with your venture. Growing your leadership is a life-long process, but it takes around 3-5 years to develop the leadership skills necessary to sustain a growing business.

6. How good are you at meeting new people? If not good at all, are you willing to commit to mastering this skill? Business is all about people. Your ability to meet new business partners, mentors, clients, etc., will play an important role in expanding your reach.

7. How well do you adapt to ever-changing scenarios? Business is evolving rapidly, at a rate that has never been seen in history. A quick look at industry disruptors such as Uber, Amazon, Air BnB, etc., can verify this. A great businessman must understand what Charles Darwin understood a few hundred years ago: *"It's not the strongest species that survives, it's the quickest to adapt to changes in its environment"*.

8. How demanding are you of the people you let into your life? I don't mean this in the negative sense either. But it's necessary that those who you let into your inner circle add value to your life. If there are any toxic people in your inner circle, they will subtract energy from you. Contradicting emotions, unnecessary drama, and toxicity are the last things entrepreneurs need in order to move forward.

9. Which do you value more: security or achievement? Business is incredibly volatile and uncertain during its period of infancy. There will be times in which you may make a lot of money right away, and there will be times where you won't even be able to pay yourself. Your drive to succeed must stronger than your need for security, especially at the beginning.

10. Do you have the humility to ask for help? Or do you think you can do it all on your own? This goes back to Maxwell's saying about needing others to achieve great things. However, you must not only be a team player, you must also know when to admit you're wrong and go to others to ask for help. In whatever undertaking, there's always someone who has already gone to the top. We can save ourselves months or years of trial and error by getting help from those who've already achieved it.

11. How badly do you want it? How ecstatic do you get from visualizing your business succeed? What causes will your business represent? How intense is your desire? The greatest common denominator of all business success is *burning desire*. You have to have it.

Evaluation: If you've answered *yes* to at least 8 of the 11 questions then you've got entrepreneur material in you. I suggest that you look into entrepreneurship as a real possibility for you and start evaluating the kind of project you'd like to create. It doesn't even have to be a for-profit-business; it could be an NGO you're after. Don't have the money? Then, I'd suggest starting a part-time business while keeping your full-time job. Once you're making more money from your business, then you can quit your job. That's what I did!

Disclaimer & What this evaluation is not: Just because you didn't answer *'yes'* to all of these doesn't mean you're not cut out to be an entrepreneur. I was a want-trepreneur at age 17. At that age, I had a lot of ego (with no real basis for it), wouldn't ask others for help, was a huge loner, hated meeting people, and valued security over success. And it was true- at that age, I wasn't really ready for what I was getting into. My first relative success with business came at age 20 when I finally started making money (profit!) from a business idea I had launched. While I didn't have the skillset, I did have desire and persistence. It's these two traits that kept me going despite the setbacks and discouragement I received from friends and family. Therefore, this evaluation is not the be all, end all evaluation- I don't think there will ever be one. All that's necessary to be successful in the long-term in entrepreneurship is burning desire and persistence, as these two traits will bring about all others in due time. What this evaluation is: a measure by which to gauge if you're ready to start a business *now, at this moment.*

For Entrepreneurs!

You've decided it! Entrepreneurship is for you, and you're not going to let anything stop you. Perfect! In the following questions, we will ask you to analyze possible ventures an ideas that will take into account all the things we've covered thus far. Note that this is also applicable if you're trying to start a non-profit.

12. Taking into consideration what we've talked about purpose, identity (including skills and capabilities), and values, make a list of all the possible business ideas that you'd like to develop that would be in alignment with each one of these aspects about yourself. Take your time with this list, you're welcome to make it as long as possible.

13. Hope you have a lot of ideas written down. Narrow down this list by making your top ten favorite business ideas.

14. Next to each business idea, describe *why* you'd be willing to start it. Is your *why* compelling enough?

15. Next to each business idea, describe the *value* you'd be giving your clients (or the problem you're trying to solve for them). Does solving this particular problem resonate with you?

16. Next to each business idea, describe the *reward* you'd get from starting and growing it. Does the *reward* excite you?

17. Next to each business idea, describe why people should choose *you* above all other competitors? What makes *you* stand out?

Having answered all of these questions will narrow the list down to only a few candidates. The only three remaining factors to analyze are the market, resources, and your ability to leverage your efforts.

18. To evaluate the market ask yourself: Is there a real demand for what I'm doing? How easily can I enter the market?

19. As for resources: what resources would you need to start this project? If you don't have them all, what's the minimum required to just *start*?

20. As for leverage: is your project scalable? What actions can you take now (and during the process of starting your business) that will have the most effect on it long term?

21. Finally, what business path have you chosen?

For Professionals!

None of that entrepreneurial nonsense- you're more the kind who wants to craft their skill and take it to the highest level. Great stuff. To narrow down the vehicle you use to fulfill your purpose, answer the following questions.

22. Taking into account your purpose, identity, and values, what skill or ability that you can put into the service of others do you want to commit to mastering? Make a list of at least 5 of these.

23. Next to each of the skills or abilities, detail who you'd want to do them for. *E.g. NGOs, large corporations, individuals, agencies, political groups, etc.* Choose one entity that resonates with you.

24. Next to each of the skills or abilities, detail the need or the want you will satisfy of the client/organization/individual you mentioned above.

25. Ask yourself: how does this entity change as a result? Does being responsible for this change excite me?

26. After having examined and evaluated your top five skills and abilities, complete the following writing prompt. *The vehicle I have chosen to fulfill my purpose is…*

Step 5: The Making of a Legacy

The secret to living an extraordinary life: to actively craft the legacy you want to leave behind through your actions. My mentor used to say, *"Most people's lives revolve around eating, shi**ing, and sleeping. It's no wonder that no one remembers them after they die"*. It's raw, a bit offensive, but ultimately true. Only the people who actively crafted their legacy in life can be remembered. We all hold a belief that our life must have some kind of meaning. If not, it wouldn't be worth living. Through the years, I have learned that there's no better person to designate this meaning other than yourself.

- *But Gerald, haven't we covered the questions about legacy already?*
- *Yes.*

But, you see, it's also the question that we finish this process of self-discovery with. Once you've found your designated vehicle, you must ask whether it really is the best option through which you'll fulfill your life's purpose.

1. Can this vehicle set me off on the right path towards accomplishing my life's purpose?

2. Would you be proud of the legacy you'd leave behind if you chose this vehicle as your only means towards fulfilling your mission?

3. Note that the vehicle you use to fulfill your purpose can change at different stages of your life. What's important is if the vehicle you're choosing is correct for you *now*. Is this the correct vehicle for fulfilling my life's purpose *at this very moment*?

Conclusion: The Secret Step to Living with Passion

Congrats for making it this far! Now comes the important part: *Action*.

Action is the most key component to living with passion. There could be an activity that is in alignment with your purpose, identity, and values, however, if you're not putting in the effort to master your craft, then it will never develop into a passion. I'll let you in on a little secret- it's repetition, focus, and massive action that turns an activity into a passion, not the other way around. So, don't wait, don't procrastinate, and decide to take action immediately on the discoveries you've made by completing this workbook.

How I Discovered My Passion

All my life growing up, I suffered from poor self-esteem and had a very pessimistic outlook on what would become my future. Very deep down, though, I knew I wanted to be of positive impact on the lives of others. Opportunity came knocking on my door a few days after my 18th birthday. I was presented with a network marketing business opportunity and saw the possibility of making some much-needed extra cash on the side. I accepted right away as I was barely making ends meet as a college sophomore. I decided to become coachable and learn from the person who sponsored me and from the company's educational system. What happened later became a nearly life-changing experience for me. I began listening to audios of successful people, started reading books about successful people, and assisting conferences where successful people gathered. This was a kind of association that I had never experienced before in my life. Soon, the way I thought and acted changed. I began seeing a puzzle unfold before my eyes.

At first, I only did network marketing for the money. I saw young people my age who were financially free and never had to work again. I desperately wanted a life like theirs. However, as I grew in rank and team volume, I began seeing my daily network marketing activities as a powerful vehicle for achieving my purpose. For as long as I can remember I've always wanted to inspire others to believe more in themselves. This is, in part, because I wish I could've had someone to serve as my inspiration during my teenage years. With every new recruit that joined my business, I saw myself playing the role of a mentor and leader. I had to create a genuine friendship with each one of them, empower them, and teach them through example how the business worked. Some people entered the business with ridiculously low self-esteem, others with ridiculously high egos. Nevertheless, it was my job the guide them and forge leadership qualities in each one of them.

Network marketing soon became a vehicle that was in alignment with my purpose, values, beliefs- and eventually, my skills and talents. Starting out, I had zero leadership qualities, I stuttered when speaking in front of a crowd, and I lacked basic communication skills. However, because the idea of helping others to believe in themselves (specifically in their ability to lead masses and create financial freedom) was so *exciting* for me, I learned to develop these skills. It didn't take long for me to find myself standing in crowds of thousands of people sharing my story.

Before *discovering* my passion, I was aware very aware of the network marketing business model but had never paid much attention to it. I knew you had to create a team of consumers and distributors and that you could generate passive income from their consumption or sales- it just didn't seem appealing to me at all. Without having *put in the necessary action* I would've never discovered that this was my passion. Always remember that *action begets passion*, not the other way around.

Having said that there are two possible scenarios that may have resulted from you finding your vehicle through this workbook. First, your vehicle may be something that you anticipated, and thus you may have found yourself in familiar territory. If that's the case, passion may be easier to develop. If, however, the vehicle you've found is something you didn't expect, then don't knock it until you try it. Be willing to give it chance. Try, experiment, live. There is no right or wrong, there is no time limit. I always push my friends, business partners, and downlines to do everything in urgency, but never in a rush- there's a difference. Take action with abandon, with urgency. But, also know deep down that it's okay to make mistakes. So, go ahead, begin planning your next move. This may very well be the start of the legacy you'll leave behind.

References

- Vance, Ashlee. Elon Musk: Tesla, SpaceX, And The Quest For A Fantastic Future. : . Print.

- Maxwell, John C. The 17 Indisputable Laws of Teamwork: Embrace Them and Empower Your Team. Nashville: T. Nelson, 2001. Print.

- Aileron. "The Only Entrepreneur Test You Will Ever Need." Forbes, Forbes Magazine, 4 June 2012, www.forbes.com/sites/aileron/2012/06/04/the-only-entrepreneur-test-you-will-ever-need/#358d001a3af7.

- Davenport, Barrie. "15 Probing Questions to Help You Bust Through Limiting Beliefs." Expert Enough, expertenough.com/2959/15-probing-questions-to-help-you-bust-through-limiting-beliefs.

- "What Are Your Values?: Deciding What's Most Important in Life." From MindTools.com, www.mindtools.com/pages/article/newTED_85.htm.

- "How to Discover Your Mission, Values, Purpose and Legacy." Asian Efficiency, 13 Aug. 2015, www.asianefficiency.com/systems/discover-mission-values-purpose-legacy/.

- "15 Questions That Reveal Your Ultimate Purpose in Life." Goodlife Zen, 16 Mar. 2018, goodlifezen.com/15-questions-that-reveal-your-ultimate-purpose-in-life/.

-

Made in the USA
Middletown, DE
29 September 2019